YOUR KNOWLEDGE HAS VALUE

- We will publish your bachelor's and master's thesis, essays and papers

- Your own eBook and book - sold worldwide in all relevant shops

- Earn money with each sale

Upload your text at www.GRIN.com and publish for free

Bibliographic information published by the German National Library:

The German National Library lists this publication in the National Bibliography; detailed bibliographic data are available on the Internet at http://dnb.dnb.de .

This book is copyright material and must not be copied, reproduced, transferred, distributed, leased, licensed or publicly performed or used in any way except as specifically permitted in writing by the publishers, as allowed under the terms and conditions under which it was purchased or as strictly permitted by applicable copyright law. Any unauthorized distribution or use of this text may be a direct infringement of the author s and publisher s rights and those responsible may be liable in law accordingly.

Imprint:

Copyright © 2017 GRIN Verlag
Print and binding: Books on Demand GmbH, Norderstedt Germany
ISBN: 9783668675230

This book at GRIN:

https://www.grin.com/document/418735

Max Bailey

"Atmosfear" and Rising Populism. Climate Change in Society

GRIN Verlag

GRIN - Your knowledge has value

Since its foundation in 1998, GRIN has specialized in publishing academic texts by students, college teachers and other academics as e-book and printed book. The website www.grin.com is an ideal platform for presenting term papers, final papers, scientific essays, dissertations and specialist books.

Visit us on the internet:

http://www.grin.com/

http://www.facebook.com/grincom

http://www.twitter.com/grin_com

'Atmosfear' has eroded the public's confidence in climate science, combining with underlying anger at the 'establishment' to create a populist environment unconducive to meaningful climate action.

2016 will be remembered as the year in which populism once more became a powerful political force. Although the election of Donald Trump and the Brexit referendum were undoubtedly the stand out political events of this year, the rise of populist parties across Europe demonstrate that this political shift is not limited to the Anglosphere. This rise in populism serves as a reflection of the public's anger and disillusionment with mainstream political parties, and the railings of populists against the 'metropolitan elite' resonate within countries facing an ever increasing disparity in wealth. The politicised nature of climate change means that the election of these populists will inevitably hinder climate policy, as Giddens warns of in his book 'Politics and Climate Change' [1], because governments may attempt to appease this growing faction by reducing action on climate change. The opposition of populists to action on global emissions stems in part from the historic use of 'atmosfear', which has eroded the public's confidence in climate science, and populists have seized upon this to differentiate themselves from mainstream political parties. The politicisation of climate change led it to be inextricably linked to mainstream political parties, and as a result some oppose climate policies simply due to the support it receives from the 'establishment' "we have all become more confused, more wary, more questioning and perhaps even distrustful of science and authority in general" [2]. This underlying sense of suspicion towards major international organisations and the political process could not have come at a worse time, as any global response which a solution to climate change mandates is now seen as an attempt by political institutions to expand their power, and therefore any solution would be met with opposition from a disenfranchised populace.

Climate change dominates much of the news cycle, with a continual stream of articles discussing the devastating impacts that it will bring. However for all the predictions of impeding destruction in popular media, most famously the "true planetary emergency" discussed in Al Gore's 2006 documentary 'An Inconvenient Truth' [3], there has been little noticeable impact on people in many developed countries. This is one of the most unjust consequences of climate change, in that it mainly affects those who contributed least to it, leaving the major polluters with no visible incentive to change. Thus when attempting to communicate the potential impacts of climate change, politicians and scientists alike have often resorted to the hyperbolic, with the media given select soundbites to warn of the 'extreme weather events' that climate change can cause in an attempt to galvanise the public into action. The appeal of using this 'atmosfear' when discussing the potential impacts of climate change stems from the four main advantages it provides [4]. By reducing the complexity of climate change to the easily observable impacts of weather extremes, 'atmosfear' provides a clearly identifiable issue which can be targeted for resolution. The devastating effects that these catastrophic weather events wreak on both ecosystems and society demand a unified response through the form of enacted climate policy, as government intervention is necessary for the final goal of a carbon free society to be attained. The unifying theme behind these statements is that a "non-anthropogenic climate – is assumed to be more benign than an anthropogenically influenced one" [5], and therefore a return to a pre-industrial climate is the desired end goal of any actions undertaken.

However there are multiple issues associated with the use of 'atmosfear' to communicate findings in climate science. Using 'atmosfear' to frame the discussion around climate change oversimplifies the issue, and in some instances exaggerates or even falsifies the science. "Weather extremes are only one of the predicted effects of climate change and are best addressed by measures other than emission policies" [6], and therefore it is disingenuous to state that solving climate change will lead to a future free from such events. Furthermore, when there is a lack of extreme weather events, it discredits the arguments that are integral to 'atmosfear', and by extension discredits climate change as a whole. If climate change is to be defined by its visible effects, and for many citizens there are none, then the implication is that climate change is therefore not a significant issue. The rhetoric of 'atmosfear' also implies that the condition of the climate is such that it must be reverted to pre-industrial norms for society to be safe from weather extremes, yet in reality this goal is unattainable due to the advanced state of emissions[7].

This dependency on 'atmosfear', the "assumptions that link climate change to severe weather events in ways in which such events become signifiers of a peril that goes beyond their limited individual impact" [8], has as a result had the opposite effect intended, with the media reporting that the public has begun to show signs of what they have come to term "green fatigue" [9]. By this they mean that developments in climate science are no longer registering interest, and are even seen by some as unreliable. This disinterest in climate change has coincided with a growing disillusionment with the general trustworthiness of politicians and the media, compounding the problems facing the attainment of any political solution to climate change. The nature of climate change as a 'wicked problem', a problem which "involves the phenomena, decisions, values and uncertainties that are at once natural and social and that require urgent action on matters involving highest stakes" [10], also means that any solution to the issue will require global cooperation, and populists have seized upon this to rail against a liberal, utopian ideal of a global society, feeding off the resentment of working class voters left behind by globalisation to obtain their support.

That is not to say that the media has only advanced the arguments of mainstream parties and cohesive climate action. The election of Donald Trump can in large part be attributed to the practice of providing air time to whomever attracts an audience, regardless of the content "the media gave Trump far too much unfiltered airtime" [11]. Furthermore, the tendency of the mainstream media to attempt to present a 'balanced' viewpoint by providing space for both sides of the argument has enhanced the reputability of climate scepticism. This adherence to 'Journalistic Tradition' [12], coupled with the actions of certain news corporations dedicated to forwarding climate scepticism, most notably Rupert Murdoch's Fox News, where "debunking climate science is official policy" [13], has led to climate change scepticism now being a respectable position to hold in certain circles.

The arguments put forward by the climate change deniers, at times indistinguishable from those proposed by conspiracy theorists, have in part been able to flourish due to the rhetoric used by the 'establishment' when discussing climate change. The failure of some of the most catastrophic of warnings to materialise, such as the report by Professor Wieslaw Maslowski in 2007, which had a "projection for the removal of ice in summer" in the Arctic by 2013 [14] have supported the arguments of sceptics, by lending credence to the notion that the claims of scientists are grossly exaggerated, and that the issue of climate change is greatly overblown. This argument was greatly strengthened by the 'Climategate' scandal, where leaked emails from the Climatic Research Unit at the University of East Anglia suggested that parties central to the IPCC and Michael Mann's famous 'hockey stick' graph discussed how to avoid releasing data to the public. The emails furthermore alluded to 'attempts' to manipulate data to fit it to preconceived models, significantly impacting upon public confidence in climate science. [15]

The impact of these controversies has been reflected in the growth of climate scepticism amongst the public "according to a new survey, one in five people deny that temperatures are rising at all, with only just over 50% convinced that man-made climate change is real" [16], despite an ever increasing amount of evidence to the contrary. There was a demonstrable rise in climate scepticism in the UK between 2009 and 2010, with a 'Populus' poll finding an increase from 15% to 25% of those who disagreed with the statement that "do you think global warming is taking place". This is a clear example of the impact that the media can have on influencing public perceptions, as the survey was undertaken during the period surrounding the 'Climategate' controversy on the 17th of November, 2009. There was also a significant drop over this period of those that agreed that climate change existed and was "established as largely man made", from 41% to 26% [17]. Although the emails were later explained as being taken out of context by those involved "one cherry picked email has gone viral... I was not questioning the link between anthropogenic greenhouse gas emissions and warming..."[18], the way in which media outlets reported the leaks caused significant damage to the scientific community by undermining the trust that the public had in scientists. Thus concerted attacks from right leaning publications have also been responsible for the rise in climate scepticism, and combined with the lefts tendency of resorting to 'atmosfear', a polarised media environment has ensued, hampering attempts to reach common ground for action against climate change.

In contrast to its relationship with the media, climate change is not specifically on the agenda for many populist political parties. With the exception of Donald Trump, who actively campaigned on a platform advocating the return to 'clean coal' to court the votes of the coal country[19], most populist parties pay minimum lip service to the question of environmental policy. Some parties such as UKIP do see through climate change scepticism the opportunity to differentiate themselves from mainstream political parties, but it is not a cornerstone policy. However, climate change's requirement for a global solution flies directly in the face of the nationalist policies and the rhetoric that populist parties employ - the belief that a nation is best able to resolve issues through internal actions, and that isolationist policies are key to a nation's success. [20] Thus by delegitimising climate change through scepticism, they aim to remove a key political issue which requires international cooperation. As a result, climate change is most commonly discussed by populists through the lens of an opportunity to attack the globalist policies of a so called 'metropolitan elite', whose lectures on the evils of the daily actions of the public with respect to their environmental impact creating a sense of being bullied by an out of touch upper class. Returning to Donald Trump, his shift in attitude towards climate change makes an interesting case study. Before announcing his intentions for politics, he was a signatory to a letter to President Obama urging him to "lead the world by example" [21] in efforts against climate change. We therefore see that climate scepticism can be utilised as a tactic to obtain votes, indicating an underlying level of discontent towards the current climate policies of mainstream political parties, or at least at their perceived effects.

Populists often target the support of those who feel 'left behind' by society, and climate change is a topic which coincides with this aim. Climate policies whose impacts result in rising energy costs disproportionately affect those on lower incomes, and what an urbanite may consider an insignificant 10% rise in energy costs can be a significant blow to the finances of a low income household. Furthermore, policies which aim to promote the purchase of green energy and low carbon devices often act as a direct subsidy to the upper middle classes. With the Government's Renewable Heat Incentive, the purchase of a Biomass boiler has the potential to return 65% on investment according to Euroheat [22]. However the boiler in this instance costs £35,000, a sum far beyond the reach of most households, and therefore only the wealthiest can take advantage of the up to £24,500 in subsidies offered by the government. With the financial impacts that enacted climate policy can bring, with subsidies aimed at the rich and costs which disproportionately affect the poor, it is understandable why there is significant resentment towards certain climate policies and the additional costs that they bring

Climate scepticism amongst political parties is not exclusive to the Anglosphere. Even in Europe, where national governments have often been at the forefront for action against climate change, there has been some fightback against climate policies. The AfD and Front National focus on the international relationships that the solutions to climate change require, particularly within the framework of the EU, and are able to gain popular support for their opposition to climate policies by pointing to the significant rises in energy prices and impact that this has on industry competitiveness. [23] This is illustrated by the consequences of the Energiewende programme in Germany, legislatively passed in 2010, recently calculated to have an estimated total cost of up to 520 billion euros in the years leading up to 2025 according to the University of Düsseldorf. This figure was in stark contrast to the predictions of the Environmental Minister Peter Altmaier 3 years previously, and has been a source of significant controversy, reinforcing the view of politicians as being deceptive. [24] Thus in Germany, a country where the manufacturing sector provides a pathway to wealth for many from lower income backgrounds [25], fears of the potential impacts on jobs that climate policies forwarded by the 'establishment' can have has helped the AfD. However the bulk of the support for these two parties stems from anger at the EU and towards the mass immigration currently taking place, both of which fit into a 'liberal utopia' of borderless societies and individual freedoms. Thus by adding climate scepticism to their policies, they are able to support their principle arguments against globalism.

Through the success of populist parties and their disproportionate popularity amongst lower income households, the question arises as to whether climate change in the western world is a quintessentially middle class issue. People struggling to make ends meet have more pressing issues than the potential for 'some polar ice caps' to melt, and the intangible effects of climate change are in stark contrast to the significant rises in energy prices that can result from climate policies. The subsidies put in place to mitigate emissions also predominantly benefit those from wealthier backgrounds. However it is deceptive to paint lower income households and populists as the only source of opposition to political intervention against climate change. Libertarian ideals have become increasingly popular alongside isolationist rhetoric, despite being polar opposites in principle and traditional support base. In the 2016 US presidential elections, Gary Johnson, representing the libertarian party, garnered over 4 million votes (3.2% of the vote)[26], which may seem insignificant, but was in fact more than the previous eight libertarian presidential tickets combined. Although some of this can be attributed to the universal unpopularity of the Republican and Democrat candidates, support for a decreasing role of government in society has risen as a result of a series of disastrous interventions from the government. Libertarian opposition to climate change action, such as the CATO institute which "has been waging a media war against the very notion for years" [27], poses a significant problem as the free market solutions supported by libertarians have been demonstrably unsuccessful, with the failure of the CDM and other capitalistic mechanisms evidence that these theories do not work in practice [28]. By splitting the vote previously reserved for mainstream parties, they also help create a path for populists to power [29] and hence create new blockages to the passage of climate policy.

The election of populists who hold sceptical views on climate policies poses a significant threat to any lasting solution to climate change, as the cohesive "ensuring state" which Giddens writes of in 'The Politics of Climate Change' requires a cross party consensus in order to function[30]. Giddens' amongst others argues that the politicisation of climate change has caused many of the issues facing an all-encompassing political solution incorporating the concept of "forward planning"[31], as each election cycle brings with it the risk of a complete shift in climate policy. This is particularly salient with the election of Donald Trump, who has vowed to scrap the Clean Power Act as part of his "100-day action plan" [32]. Thus the media and political establishment, in creating an environment in which populist parties have been able to thrive, have significantly damaged any chances of obtaining a unified political solution to climate change. It is furthermore possible that the number of climate sceptics is higher than reported, as it is seen as an unorthodox and unacceptable view that people may feel uncomfortable admitting to holding, as in the Brexit referendum and the US Presidential election. The at times derogatory manner in which climate scepticism is discussed may even harden views on climate change by fostering an 'us vs them' siege mentality, an issue made worse by the general wealth disparity between climate sceptics and believers. Thus efforts must be made to not resort to ad hominin when debating climate sceptics, but rather deconstruct their arguments, in order to educate the populace on the issues facing the planet. Otherwise the message of the unstoppable nature of climate change will never reach the necessary sceptics, and there will be an increasing polarisation between the two sides. By changing the dialogue around climate change to move away from hyperbole and insult, climate scepticism might be effectively addressed.

In conclusion, the way in which climate change has been framed by the media and mainstream political parties has created a highly polarised debate. This has combined with an underlying distrust in the trustworthiness of the media and politicians, fuelling a rise in scepticism. The use of 'atmosfear' to communicate the potential impacts of climate change has led to suspicions of deception, denting the public's confidence in the genuine evidence supporting anthropogenic climate change. The rise of populist parties can also in part be attributed to the suppression of rational debate and the normalisation of hyperbole, seen at times in the discussion surrounding climate change. In this environment populist policies have resonated with a disenfranchised populace left financially behind by globalisation, suspicious of attempts to create the closer ties between nations necessary for combating rising emissions. The rise in populism thus poses a direct threat to unified action against climate change, as the nationalist tendencies of populists directly conflict with the global solutions required for climate change mitigation.[33] To combat this rise, efforts ought to be made to detoxify both the political environment and the debate surrounding climate change. The reintroduction of rational discourse in the political sphere could address some of the concerns of reluctant climate sceptics, whose primary concerns may centre on the potential financial impacts of climate change rather than the scientific evidence in itself. By recognising the concerns of a politically alienated populace, the platform of populist parties would also be suffocated, potentially leading to the cross party consensus necessary for long term climate change mitigation strategies.

1 Giddens, Anthony. The Politics of Climate Change, Polity Press (2009): 15

2 Sinanian, Arek. "Climate Change and the Distrust of Authority". Fair Observer. 22 February. (2016) http://www.fairobserver.com/more/environment/climate-change-and-the-distrust-of-authority-53405/ (accessed November 23, 2016).

3 Gore, Albert A. Jr. An Inconvenient Truth. DVD. Directed by Davis Guggenheim. Paramount Pictures: Paramount Classics, 2006.

4 Jankovic, V., and D. Schultz, 2016: Atmosfear: Communicating the Effects of Climate Change on Extreme Weather. Wea. Climate Soc. doi:10.1175/WCAS-D-16-0030.1, in press: 2

5 Jankovic, V., and D. Schultz, 2016: Atmosfear: Communicating the Effects of Climate Change on Extreme Weather. Wea. Climate Soc. doi:10.1175/WCAS-D-16-0030.1, in press: 2

6 Jankovic, V., and D. Schultz, 2016: Atmosfear: Communicating the Effects of Climate Change on Extreme Weather. Wea. Climate Soc. doi:10.1175/WCAS-D-16-0030.1, in press: 2

7 Jankovic, V., and D. Schultz, 2016: Atmosfear: Communicating the Effects of Climate Change on Extreme Weather. Wea. Climate Soc. doi:10.1175/WCAS-D-16-0030.1, in press: 15-16

8 Jankovic, V., and D. Schultz, 2016: Atmosfear: Communicating the Effects of Climate Change on Extreme Weather. Wea. Climate Soc. doi:10.1175/WCAS-D-16-0030.1, in press: 8

9 Moser, Susanne C. Communicating climate change: History, challenges, process and future directions Wiley Interdisciplinary Reviews-Climate Change, 1 (1) (2010) 43

10 Jankovic, V., and D. Schultz, 2016: Atmosfear: Communicating the Effects of Climate Change on Extreme Weather. Wea. Climate Soc. doi:10.1175/WCAS-D-16-0030.1, in press: 21

11 Sillito, David. "Donald Trump: How the media created the president". BBC. 14 November. (2016) http://www.bbc.co.uk/news/entertainment-arts-37952249 (accessed November 25, 2016).

12 Moser, Susanne C. Communicating climate change: History, challenges, process and future directions Wiley Interdisciplinary Reviews-Climate Change, 1 (1) (2010) 32

13 Hamilton, Clive. "Silencing the Scientists: the Rise of Right-wing Populism" UN University: Australian National Unviersity. 03 February. (2011) http://ourworld.unu.edu/en/silencing-the-scientists-the-rise-of-right-wing-populism (accessed November 24, 2016).

14 Amos, Jonathon. "Arctic summers ice-free 'by 2013'" BBC. 12 December. (2007) http://news.bbc.co.uk/1/hi/7139797.stm (accessed November 25, 2016).

15 Booker, Christopher. "Climate change: this is the worst scientific scandal of our generation" The Telegraph. 28 November. (2009) http://www.telegraph.co.uk/comment/columnists/christopherbooker/6679082/Climate-change-this-is-the-worst-scientific-scandal-of-our-generation.html (accessed November 18, 2016)

16 "UN confronts rise of climate change denial" The Day. 23 September. (2013) https://theday.co.uk/environment/climate-change-deniers-on-the-rise-says-un (accessed November 20, 2016)

17 "Climate scepticism 'on the rise', BBC poll shows" BBC. 07 February. (2010) http://news.bbc.co.uk/1/hi/8500443.stm (accessed November 20, 2016)

18 Trenberth, Kevin. Statement: Kevin Trenberth on Hacking of Climate Files. CGD's Climate Analysis Section (CAS). National Centre for Atmospheric Research (2010)

19 Lederman, Josh. "Courting coal country, Trump vows to put miners back to work" The Washington Post, AP. 10 August. (2016) https://www.washingtonpost.com/politics/courting-coal-country-trump-vows-to-put-

miners-back-to-work/2016/08/10/ca84aa5e-5f47-11e6-84c1-6d27287896b5_story.html (accessed November 21, 2016)

20 Rachman, Gideon. "Marine Le Pen, climate and the defeat of nationalism" Financial Times, 14 December. (2015) https://www.ft.com/content/e9039db8-a247-11e5-bc70-7ff6d4fd203a (accessed November 23, 2016)

21 Meyer, Robinson. "A Yuuuuuge Climate Flip Flop" The Atlantic, 10 June. (2016) http://www.theatlantic.com/science/archive/2016/06/trump-climate-change-new-york-times-letter-ad/486335/ (accessed 21 November, 2016)

22 Blackmore, Nicole "Could you earn a 65pc return from a biomass boiler?" The Independent, 25 August. (2014) http://www.telegraph.co.uk/finance/personalfinance/energy-bills/11050580/Could-you-earn-a-65pc-return-from-a-wood-burning-biomass-boiler.html (accessed 27 November, 2016)

23 Knight, Ben "What does the AfD stand for?" Deutsche Welle, 07 March. (2016) http://www.dw.com/en/what-does-the-afd-stand-for/a-19100127 (accessed 21 November 2016)

24 Wetzel, Daniel "Energiewende kostet die Bürger 520.000.000.000 Euro – erstmal" Die Welt, 10 October. (2016) https://www.welt.de/wirtschaft/article158668152/Energiewende-kostet-die-Buerger-520-000-000-000-Euro-erstmal.html (accessed 27 November, 2016, Source in German)

25 Carapezza, Kirk and Noe-Payne Mallory " 'Blue collar aristocrats' thrive in German economy" Marketplace, 07 April. (2015) http://www.marketplace.org/2015/04/07/education/learning-curve/blue-collar-aristocrats-thrive-german-economy (accessed 03 December, 2016)

26 Dwilson, Stephanie D. "How many votes did Gary Johnson get in the presidential election?" Heavy, 10 November. (2016) http://heavy.com/news/2016/11/how-many-votes-electoral-did-gary-johnson-get-in-the-presidential-election-libertarian/ (accessed 25 November, 2016)

27 Pigliucci, Massimo. "Why do libertarians deny climate change?" Rationally Speaking (blog), 27 May. (2010) http://rationallyspeaking.blogspot.co.uk/2010/05/why-do-libertarians-deny-climate-change.html (accessed 03 December, 2016)

28 Böhm, Steffen. "Why are carbon markets failing?" The Guardian, 12 April. (2013) https://www.theguardian.com/sustainable-business/blog/why-are-carbon-markets-failing (accessed 10 December, 2016)

29 Smith, Reiss. "Who is Gary Johnson – the Libertarian Party candidate who could win US election for Trump" Express UK, 05 November. (2016) http://www.express.co.uk/news/world/729045/gary-johnson-who-is-libertarian-party-us-election-2016-win-trump (accessed 08 December, 2016)

30 Giddens, Anthony. The Politics of Climate Change, Polity Press (2009): 15

31 Giddens, Anthony. The Politics of Climate Change, Polity Press (2009): 8

32 D. J. Trump, An America First Energy Plan, Address, North Dakota, 26 May. (2016) https://www.theguardian.com/sustainable-business/blog/why-are-carbon-markets-failing (accessed 09 December, 2016)

33 Norton, Andrew. "Climate denial and the populist right" International Institute for Environment and Development, 15 November. (2016) http://www.iied.org/climate-denial-populist-right (accessed 10 December, 2016)

YOUR KNOWLEDGE HAS VALUE

- We will publish your bachelor's and master's thesis, essays and papers

- Your own eBook and book - sold worldwide in all relevant shops

- Earn money with each sale

Upload your text at www.GRIN.com
and publish for free